The North Wind

Book Two of
The Tin Train Series

By Norma Jean

Denty Publications

dentypuublishing.com

Contents

Karen's Memoirs

"Look to God and pray my child that good people can influence your life."

Ella Loree (Lamb) Baas

When we were children, our parents loved us. However, because of our fathers drinking problem his wife and children suffered much pain, physical and emotional abuse.

Our mother's small and fragile body and mind was stripped of all dignity. There were no laws to protect her.

Pregnant and babe in arms, toddlers, and growing children underfoot, grabbed by her hair both eyes blackened, Dad had gotten drunk, he was an alcoholic. When dad would come home mother was grabbed, dragged, pulled, and beaten. She was carried into the bathroom; her small and fragile body was forced over the tub, while my father whipped out his manhood and put it into her. She was sometimes eight months pregnant.

How do we know, we were there. We saw it all happen time and time again. We would all start to cry because dad was hurting her.

Why are we telling all this, because we must heal our minds? Maybe perhaps we want to help someone else, from making the same mistakes.

All the family and friends must have known because they quit coming around. No one wanted to get involved. Even if they would have tried to help it would have made the beatings, the suffering, the pain that much harder on all of us.

Karen (Baas) Worline

Dedication

I dedicate this book to my three brothers who have already gone to be with Jesus in heaven.

John, you are the most recent who has gone from this life to the next. May God keep you safe in His ever-loving arms.

You had it rough, because our parents would not curtail your bad habits. They made them come alive repeatedly. They never gave you any discipline so that you might know right from wrong. They would brag about your escapades instead.

Daryl, you were the first of all of us to go. You were our youngest brother. I promised you years ago, I would tell our story and let everyone know what we went through as children. It has been fifteen years since your passing. I am finally getting the courage to write our story. It has been scary putting all this out there for all to see but I did promise you I would. Your good nature and gentle spirit never stood a chance in the evils of this world. You never could stand up against the onslaught of evil.

Junior, you were the oldest of all of us. You never had a chance to have a childhood. I am sorry you too had so much responsibility so early. You tried to take care of our dad and all of us by supporting us financially. You were the responsible one. However, our dad should have been taking care of you. Instead, you tried to take care of the whole family.

Preface

Some may find this book more intense than my first book. This is because I was older when the events in this book occurred and my memories of the events are much more vivid. My memory of what took place is broader. I remember more of what transpired in the years living with our grandma. Grandma Lamb was a live wire. She believed boys were the best, just like Grandma Baas. Unlike Grandma Baas, she was willing to try some girls, to see their mettle. However, not all girls could measure up.

This book takes place where my previous book left off. It begins with Grandma moving in after our mother died. For our dad to continue to raise so many kids, he needed help. Grandma supplied that help.

However, Grandma brought a completely new set of rules. She brought on a totally new set of abuses.

Grandma Comes To Stay

I spent the summer in a fog. All of my brothers and sisters were also in a fog. We were in a depression of despair and just could not seem to get out. With our mother gone, things were just not the same anymore. We did not have fun anymore. We tried to have fun but it seemed impossible. We missed our mother dearly.

Grandma moved into the back bedroom upstairs. We lived in a two-bedroom house. Junior the oldest boy was still the responsible one. He now slept in the living room with our dad. Larry usually did not have much to say also slept in the living room. John too slept in the living room downstairs. Dad and Mother used to sleep here in the living room. They slept either on the hide a bed or on the sofa bed. Freddie and Jimmy started sleeping down here on the floor in the living room. Vera slept in the back bedroom in a single bed. Daryl was the baby when our mother died. He had spent so little time with our mother, also slept with Grandma Lamb in the back bedroom in a double bed. The rest of us girls slept in two double beds in the front bedroom. The front bedroom was the larger of the two bedrooms.

Mother died at the end of May. When she died, she seemed to take our lifeblood with her. I cannot remember finishing first grade. I must have because in the fall I was in the second grade. I remember Grandma Lamb saying to me, "Norma what happened to you? You used to be clean all the time. Now you are dirty all the time." I did not understand what she was questioning. My Mother just died. I did not know how to be happy. As for being clean, I did not care if I looked clean anymore. Mother always reminded me to wash my face when it was dirty. She used to have me wash my younger brothers and sisters faces as well.

I was as tall as my older brothers and sisters. I was much taller than the younger ones as well. Everyone forgot how young I really was. They kept giving me more and more responsibility. I always followed through for them. I became proficient at everything I did. It was easier this way. Than no one noticed me. I could hide in the background. I do not know why God wanted me to be so proficient at everything. That is exactly what He did for me. God made me proficient. I saw something done once. The next time I could do it. I kept busy by helping out everywhere. By helping out this way, there really was no time to play.

I did not mind though there was not anyone for me to play with really! Vera had Karen and they were together all the time. Junior, Larry, and John were together all the time. Debbie and Freddie were together all the time. Jimmy, Joan, and Daryl were together all the time. I was the middle kid too young for the older ones to play with and too big to play with the younger ones. Literally, I am a good head taller than all the younger ones.

The summer is over now and I am back at school.

I am walking down the halls of my elementary school. All I hear is the poor thing! She is so tiny to have lost her Mother. The poor thing, they were talking about my little sister Debbie. Debbie did not go into first grade. They held her back in kindergarten because she was so tiny and immature. We were eighteen months apart. I had just turned seven and she would turn six in two months. Not much of an age difference but she was that much tinier than I was and petite too. I was a lot bigger. (Grandma Lamb had a name for it, Big Galoot) so it appeared she needed more protecting. I wanted to scream and tell them I had just lost my mother too but I could not. They told us how to feel, when to feel, and we could not express our feelings openly. So I cried silently. I never said anything.

Grandma Lamb, the grandma who lives with us now does not seem to like us very much. At least some of us she does not like much. She is different now that our mother is dead. She is mean. She is loud. She grabs us by our hair a lot. Especially when we do things wrong she pulls out our hair, when she grabs it. She calls me a crybaby a lot. I cannot seem to help it. I miss my mother. No one seems to understand that. No one seems to know how to tell my brothers, sisters, and I that we will be okay.

Grandma was a recovering alcoholic. She had the added pressure of not drinking as well as the stress of taking care of eleven children. She was already in her fifty's when she took on this responsibility the raising of her daughter's children, eleven children to be exact not a daunting task. Grandma did not raise her own children. Our aunt and uncle lived with other relatives. They did not have a home of their own.

Grandpa Lamb had not put aside any money to take care of their children and our grandma, his wife. If in case, she outlived him. Which she did out live her husband! He too was an alcoholic and a womanizer.

All this took place before they realized alcoholism was a disease and an addiction.

Accuses us of killing our mother

Soon after mother's funeral, her mother, Grandma Lamb, came to live with us. I am not sure why as she believed it was our fault that mother had died.

Grandma Lamb said, "If you had not been born your mother would still be alive today." I was numb. I could not believe she was saying these things to us. Grandma Lamb said, "You killed your mother." If I had known, I had killed her I would have gladly died in her place. Grandma Lamb had been here one week and already she is accusing us of killing her daughter.

Grandma was a changeling. Sometimes she would remember better times. Other times we got the distinct impression, she resented us for merely being alive. She was blaming us for our own mother's death, her daughter. Grandma did not even try to hide this from us. She would just say things like, "if Arthur your father had not had so many children your mother, my daughter would still be alive." Every time she got the chance, she would say things like, "if Arthur, your mother's husband, your Father had not abused her she would still be alive. If you had not been born my daughter, your Mother, would still be alive. You killed her."

I would think Mother I did not mean to kill you. I am sorry. I love you. I need you. I would cry silently. There was no crying allowed in our house. If someone would hear us crying we would be in trouble. Crying was a sin in our house. It took every ounce of courage we had not to cry aloud and let someone hear us. We could not let the tears fall on our cheeks. They could not see them. If they would see our tears, we would be in trouble. God heard us crying though. He did not stop it either. Nevertheless, He heard us crying. Sometimes we even felt abandoned by God. Perhaps He was hoping the adults would change, they never did.

We too were hoping and praying the adults in our lives would change, they never did.

With sayings like these, we also started blaming ourselves, blaming ourselves for killing our mother. Thinking if we had not been born she would still be alive. Some of us even tried committing suicide. We never succeeded. We were too afraid of the consequences.

They told us she died of cancer of the female organs. This only confirmed what we were thinking and what they accused us of, that we had killed her. Later, when we were adults, we found out, she actually died of colon cancer.

Grandma Lamb hated the fact that we were alive. She hated it that her daughter was dead. It seemed like she spent every waking moment telling us these things. It was pure torture. Every time she looked at us, she remembered her loss. She could not even stand to look at us most of the time. If she felt this way, why did she even come and live with us?

She said things like this continuously, "if you had not been born your mother would still be alive." Oh, God I wished I was dead instead of my mother.

I wish that she was still alive. If I had killed her, I did not mean to kill her. If I did, I am sorry. God please forgive me.

Grandma confused us by saying these things. God did not want us to kill any living thing. If I killed my mother, than I committed a very grievous sin against God

If Grandma Lamb knew how much pain she was, putting us through she never let on. We did not tell her either. I do not think she would have cared either way. By this time, we were too afraid of her to tell her anything. We were afraid of every adult in our life. Every adult in our lives disappointed us. Every adult in our lives taught us we could not trust them.

I wanted my mother back. Maybe even more than Grandma Lamb did. I felt

I was closest to her. I loved her very much. I missed her a lot. It hurt me to think that Grandma would say such horrible mean things to us, her daughter's children. I felt terrible about it. I moped around the house.

No one was able to console me. Of course no one tried to either.

It was a sad and lonely place that summer. The house was not the same. Oh! My brothers and sisters and I were the same. I mean we looked like we were the same on the outside. On the inside, we were different. We were forever changed. We were not happy. We did not play like normal kids anymore. We were always moping around. We were not crying. Fear of punishment kept us from showing tears. We did not play as we used to.

I think mother would have been sad to see us like this. She loved us that much. She wanted us to be happy not sad. Even with all the misery my Dad put her through she loved every one of us kids.

Mother loved us enough to make up the difference for his lack.

Grandma Lamb was a recovering alcoholic.

There is not anything worse for a recovering alcoholic than to be around an alcoholic. My dad was an alcoholic.

I think if Grandma Lamb could have wrung our necks, she would have. If she could have made us disappear, she would have. She was not much better than Dad was. At least he was open about the possibilities of a better life sometimes, when he was sober! He was not around much now that mother was gone. Dad spent his waking hours at the garage. He was never home.

The North Wind

Whenever the house got messy or we did something wrong, Grandma would say, "I'm gonna 'beeaat' ya like the north wind." Then she would get out one of Dad's belts and start swinging it around and around. She swung the end with the buckle around. She made us stand in a circle, chanting the whole time, "I'm gonna 'beeaat' ya like the north wind. Where ever it lands no one knows." Around and around she would swing this belt and buckle. She found out the buckle would hit us harder than the leather part of the belt. The whole time she was swinging this belt, she would chant, "I'm gonna 'beeaat' ya like North wind. Where it lands no one knows."

She figured that if one of us were guilty of making a mess, we were all guilty. BAM! The belt buckle hit me. It landed on your check. It landed on your ear. It landed on your head and it hurt. It left a huge welt. If it landed on your head, you got a huge knot on your head. Sometimes we even got a bloody lip. Sometimes we even got a black eye. Our ears would start to bleed. There would be a ringing in our ears for days. This tirade would go on for at least thirty minutes or more, until her rage was gone. I always closed by eyes. I always held my hands over my eyes too. I was afraid of going blind. The belt buckle hit me many times.

What I did not know was the shorter ones always wanted to stand next to me. I was one of the taller ones. So the belt buckle missed them entirely and struck me instead. The older ones always ducked down. No one wanted hit with the belt buckle. Oh how I hated those days when Grandma Lamb was on the warpath. When grandma was on the warpath, everybody hated it. It was not fun. It was not funny. We started calling grandma the north wind, when she was not within hearing distance.

To avoid being hit I did not know I was to duck down. I had my eyes closed.

I thought everyone my height or taller would always be hit. I was wrong. I found out years later that that just was not so. I closed my eyes, so I did not know to duck down. The older ones helped each other. Sometimes they would help the younger one. Grandma called the belt buckle her north wind. Someone was always hit no one seemed to care who it was, and grandma did not care.

Immediately the belt buckle left a huge welt on the side of your head. It bloodied your lip and swelled up so bad you could barely talk. The buckle cut your eye and made it turn black and blue. In this case, it hurt really badly! It was no fun at all. I really hated these days. This was just another reason to have one of those silent cries that you have with just yourself and God.

Sometimes I wished I could tell someone how I felt. If I could have expressed some kind of human emotion, it may have helped some. We could not show human emotion. Sometimes I wish I had some human contact to give me a hug. Someone to teach me how to love, but I never did.

It got to the point that human contact was hard for me. It sometimes still is. I never understood why. I learned that if a person touched me I would jump. I became a very jumpy child. Sometimes today, I am still very jumpy. I did not know this was not normal. I never had someone to teach me what was normal. I did not know what was not normal. If God cared, he had a funny way of showing he cared.

God did care though. He made sure the adults in our life kept us in Sunday school. God wanted us to learn about His love. He wanted us to learn about His Son's love. God also wanted us to learn of the love of the Holy Spirit. All this love sustained me as a child. So that when I became an adult, I could be a normal productive adult. I did not want to be a child abuser. God gave me the guidance to get through the rough spots in my life. This was one of those times. At this time in my life, I did not know all these things. I just knew I hated the life I was living.

"Jesus loves me this I know for the Bible tells me so." Silently I would sing this song in my head. Silently I cried. So far, none of the adults in my life showed me they could be trusted. There would be no tears or emotions allowed here.

Even the schoolteachers and the Sunday school teachers had a word for us, white trash. The older I got the more I felt it and saw this kind of treatment. They treated us differently. We were different. We smelled of cigarette smoke. We were dirty. Our teeth were rotting clean to the gums.

There was not any place in the bathroom for things like toothbrushes. Heck Dad did not have teeth. Grandma did not have teeth. Our Mother did not have teeth either. What do you need with a toothbrush? You are just going to lose your teeth anyway. The sooner the better, then it will not cost any more of our money. Not that it cost them any money anyway. We could not afford to go to the dentist.

I stayed in the children's choir. I was still listening to Carmen's voice. She still had the voice of an angel.

The fear of the north wind kept us from letting the house get dirty or messy at least until the next time.

Christmas with Grandma

Christmas was about the same as it always was except that my mother was not here this year. I missed her dearly. Grandma and Dad set up the tree with the help of my older brothers and sisters. John and I still were not old enough to help decorate the tree yet. We read the story "Twas the Night before Christmas." The younger kids fell asleep long before the story was over as always. They really tried to stay up but never succeeded.

I was seven this year. I remember though it snowed a lot. Snow was all around the rooftops and all over the yard. With Santa and his reindeer coming, we would be able to see their tracks. I could not wait. I loved Christmas. No there was not a lot of presents for us. It did not take many presents to make the living room look full. Sometimes there was that one little special thing that you had been wanting and lo and behold it would be there. How they ever knew I do not know but they did know.

This Christmas Eve there was a loud clatter and we woke up to the sound of sleigh bells and Santa saying, "Ho! Ho! Ho!" and Grandma hollering up the steps and shouting, "Santa has been here. Santa has been here. Come on down." So all of us younger kids came running down the stairs and wow what a sight.

The living room was all lit up from the Christmas lights. It was beautiful and magical all at the same time. I just wanted to breathe it all in. The house smelled of evergreen trees. The tinsel sparkled every time a breeze would capture it and if you listened carefully, you could hear the sounds of the night. We would listen to see if we could hear Santa.

Dad would put Christmas Carols on the record player and we would all sing Christmas Carols. It was fun. It was four o'clock in the morning. We unwrapped our presents too. Oh what fun it was.

Dad and Grandma tried to put on a good show for us kids but it just was not the same without our mother. Grandma and dad out did themselves. You could really tell they wanted us to not think about and be sad about our mother. However, we had learned to hide our feelings. We cried inside and pretended everything was okay.

I got an Anne Oakley outfit no doll for me this year I guess they figured I was too old for dolls. This was the best. I loved this Annie Oakley outfit. It had a holster and two guns with it. Annie Oakley was my favorite western movie character and she was a real live person. I loved John Wayne best of all but she was right up there. I could not very well pretend to be John Wayne since he was a man but I could pretend to be Anne Oakley. I loved the outfit I wore it all the time. Sometimes I even slept in my Anne

Oakley outfit. If I had not already loved western movies this would have cinched it for me.

It was the best. I wore it everywhere. I slept in my Annie Oakley outfit. I loved this Annie Oakley outfit.

Joan and Debbie both got dolls. I allowed them to play with my guns but the outfit was too big for them. The younger boys got trucks and cars to play with. We all got socks and underwear necessary items. When you had as many kids as we did it would not take very many presents to have a room full of wrapping paper. We played until we fell asleep again on the floor.

Someone had marked sleigh tracks in the snow this Christmas. There were footsteps out on the roof with sleigh tracks. There were eight sets of reindeer's paws. We could see a part of the roof from the back window it was the porch roof. It was cool to see Santa's tracks. We were all excited. It made a believer out of the most skeptics and I was just on the verge of not believing.

I remember looking at the Christmas tree with all the shimmering lights and all the tinsel that would flow in the breeze. It was so beautiful. The village with all the people placed just so around the Christmas tree. The train, the tin train was the same. The whistle blew and the light came on. The smoke stack on the engine blew its smoke too, just as it had every Christmas before. The tin train ran happily and merrily around the Christmas tree.

The village was the same too. Even though Mother was not here anymore, some things would be the same as it always was. The brass horns on the tree really worked. The little village people had movable arms and legs too.

My dad was a fanatic about Christmas. Every item on the tree had to have movable parts so his kids could play with them. We just could not break them. If we broke the ornaments, we knew we could not play with them, again. The magic would be gone for good. As Christmases past if we broke just one item then the magical spell that was Christmas would be broken. Dad would have gone off on one of his rampages and would have hit someone.

My dad was sober this year. Just like always. He promised my Mother, he would not drink anymore but that only lasted for a few months. The people who hung around my dad's garage were alcoholics too. One day they offered him a drink and he took it. That was all it took for him to be back to drinking again.

When my dad was drinking, it was scary. You just never knew who or what was going to set him off. Then he would go off in a rampage and starting hitting someone or something.

I would pray that God would make my dad stay sober but it never happened. My dad just could not stop drinking.

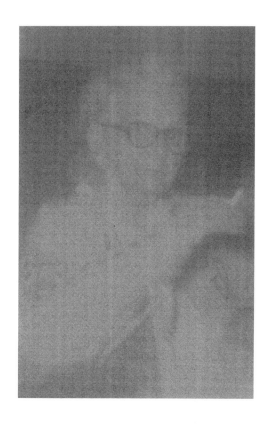

Another One of Her Tirades

"I can't hear you," Grandma hollers at the top of her lungs. Then a smack on the side of my face! She is speaking loudly this time. Another smack! I try to speak again. However, it still is not loud enough to suit her.

Grandma was a tiny woman. She may have weighed ninety pounds if she was lucky. She was only four foot nine and a half inches tall. But, she was very lean and wiry. Her hands did not have an ounce of fat on them. You could see the veins popping out in her hands. So when she smacked you it was like being smacked with a board with skin on it. She was very strong for her size. She always left a very large red welt on the side of your face. If it happened to land on your lip, your lip would start bleeding. If she hit you on the side of the head and hit your ear, it hurt badly. Your ear would start ringing or bleeding.

Grandma was having another one of her tirades. She seems to always get them when you least expected them. It was scary most of the time. This time she was having trouble hearing me. I did not understand if it was from the noise. Grandma scared me so much that I only spoke to her when I had to. Otherwise I avoided her like the plague. Nevertheless, a house with eleven kids is always going to have a lot of noise. You would think we would learn. We did not know we had to stay quiet all the time. When you have this many children in the same space day in and day out there is bound to be a lot of noise.

We even thought she was just getting hard of hearing. She proved repeatedly that just was not the case. When you did not want grandma to hear something she could hear it plainly enough.

I did try to speak louder this time. I was on the verge of tears and could not speak at all now. I tried to tell her what I had wanted to tell her and it came out as a squeak. Then she would say again, "I can't hear you." By this time, I am ready for the smack down but it did not help any, it still hurt.

She just hollers again even louder this time as if I had not heard her the first time she said it again,

"I c-a-n't h-e-a-r y-o-u.

S-p-e-a-k w-i-t-h y-o-u-r m-o-u-t-h w-i-d-e o-p-e-n."

She says it very slowly and succinctly as if she is talking to the town idiot. If I try to open my mouth now, I will start crying for sure. This time I would not be able to stop crying. To my grandma crying is a sign of weakness. I do not want to cry. Grandma has already smacked me twice, yelled at me twice. Now if I speak I know I will cry a bucket. I do not say anything at all.

If this little scenario was not enough when I did finally speak again she said, "Speak with your mouth wide open. I can't hear you." Again she said, "Speak up I can't hear you. What did you say? I can't hear you."

I was on the verge of tears, she wanted me to say what I wanted to say, and it was not coming out, it was not plain enough. She could not understand a word I was saying. Then again she said, "I can't hear you! Speak with your mouth wide open."

We never knew when grandma was going to be in one of her moods. You never knew what was going to set her off. One moment she would be one way and the next she would be entirely something else again.

Boxes Bags and Baskets

Grandma was having yet another one of her tirades. She had them a lot. This one was different than the last one. She expected an immaculate house. Well with eleven children that was not going to happen.

Grandma Lamb was like a legend. She looked as old as the hills for as long as I could remember. At fifty-four she already had white hair. She used to say, "Yes, and I earned ever' one of 'em too." She had false teeth which she wore whenever she got dressed up. She would miss-place them in the meantime. I think she would miss-place them on purpose so that she had an excuse to not have to wear them.

When she pulled her shoulders back and stood tall to her full height, she was four feet nine and a half inches tall.

She wanted to get every inch of her height out of her small frame. You knew she was on the war path. That is what we called her tirades. Grandma went from having no one at home to our house. Our house was a house full of eleven children. She promised our mother she would look after her children. She was bound and determined to see it through.

Grandma Lamb did the cooking most of the time. She did the supervising of the cleaning. We helped wherever we could. We would not dare let Grandma do it all, all by herself. When it would get really bad, Grandma Lamb would start shouting at the top of her lungs. For a tiny woman Grandma had a big, loud mouth, (you would have thought she was a drill sergeant) "Boxes, bags and baskets" and start slinging things all over the place. At first, we were so shocked. We just stood there watching. Well Grandma did not like it one bit.

We would help to clean up the place. No matter what we did it still looked messy. At first we laughed as we watched Grandma, throwing things around. It was a funny sight.

She saw us laughing and she said, "What is so funny? You think this is funny? You live like animals." She really got mad then. She took her arm drew it behind her and swung it around full force. It hit whoever was laughing. She said, "I will give you something to laugh at."

It was not funny any longer. She said, "By damned, you better never let me catch you laughing at me again. You better get them out of my sight. The next time I see boxes, bags and baskets around everywhere I will beat the living day-lights out of you." We did not laugh again that one smack that day bloodied my nose and numbed it.

Another time she hit me in the face I got a bloody lip. My lip was numb along with the side of my face. There was a hand print on the side of my faces. Another time I got hit in the head I had bells ringing in my ears. We learned real quick who was the boss and who was not.

Who was going to be in trouble and who was not going to be in trouble?

When our mother was alive, grandma was never like this. We did not know if it was because mother kept her in check or what.

It did not take long to learn in order to keep the peace in the house we had better hide all the boxes, bags and baskets. A lot of this stuff was our clothes. We had a two bedroom house. Upstairs we had at least three double beds and one single bed. There was not any room for dressers and things. Boxes of clothes could be stacked. Some could be hidden under the bed. We had one big closet in each upstairs bedroom. In each of these closets were shelves all around to put some of the boxes.

In the living room there were two couches. One folded out to a bed (hide a couch) and dad slept there along with one of the boys. The other couch (sofa bed) folded flat. It became a bed also and some of the boys slept there. Since the boys slept downstairs their clothes were downstairs where they slept. From here on out they were taken upstairs. We wanted them hidden from grandma's sight.

Some were boxes of dad's paperwork. He owned his own business. This is the reason he had paperwork all over. Dad's garage was always a mess. He could not store his paperwork at the garage. He could not have his customers looking through his paperwork. They would have taken the paperwork and he would not know who owed him money. We did not have filing cabinets for both sorting and storing this paperwork. Just to keep Grandma Lamb from going on a rampage. We started hiding the paper work.

We started hiding dad's paperwork under the buffet tables and on the landing of the basement. You would not dare loose, miss-place or hide any of dad's paperwork. He too would go on the warpath and he was worse than grandma ever was.

We learned in order to keep the peace we had to keep out of grandma's way. Sometimes it was hard to stay clear of grandma. Those of us who needed to stay out of her way helped each other to do just that.

Oh! That is to say not all of us had to stay out of her way. Her favorites did not have to they could do no wrong. They did what they wanted when they wanted and no one would be upset

.

How Disgusting Is This?

Grandma must have thought she was beyond reproach. The thing she seemed to do most often was walk around naked. She did not even seem to care who was in the house.

Grandma said, "What's the matter haven't you seen titties before?"

I was shocked and appalled that she could even say such a thing to me. Heavens yes I had seen them before but never publicly. They had never been on display before. I felt her comments were vulgar. For grandma to put them on display was bad enough but to call them her titties. I just could not believe it.

How do young girls learn modesty when the one in charge of these girls is herself walking around without modesty? My eyes must have been bugging out of my head because grandma said it again. "What's the matter haven't you seen titties before?" None of us girls could believe our eyes.

She did not even care that young impressionable boys were hanging around and watching. The boys thought it was great! Talk about buggy eyed. The boys laughed and laughed. I could not believe the boys would laugh at such a disgusting display either.

The first time I saw this I could not believe my eyes. No one else could either. It did not matter which of the kids were home. Even if the boys were home, she would do this. After a bath, she would parade around the house while looking for a towel.

You would think with this many kids around she would have taken a towel with her. She did not take a towel with her. Then I remembered the towels were in the cupboard in the bathroom. She was looking for her underwear and bra.

First thing in the morning while she was getting dressed we got a show. She took a bath in the afternoon too some days. The same thing happened she paraded around naked. There was also the evening display with all the lights on and the blinds wide open. She was on display for the whole neighborhood. You never knew what time of day she was going to take a bath and when you were going to get a show.

She walked around the house until she found what she had been looking for. The blinds in the windows would be wide open. The curtains would be wide open. Anyone walking down the street could have seen her. She seemed to be oblivious to the effects it had on us kids. If you had friends come over or walk by, with the window open it was embarrassing for them to see her like this.

Doing this did not teach us any modesty. It did not teach us to respect her. It did not show us how to respect ourselves either.

Her titties as she called them hung down to her belly button. They were sagging that much. Oh, how disgusting! No wonder the boys laughed. It left an impression on me. I could barely take my clothes off. If someone was around there was no way I was going to take off my clothes. Today if the sun goes down I cannot leave even one blind open. I do not want the neighbors gawking. The neighbors probably would not be gawking, but it is just the feeling you get.

If she paraded around like this with dad, I cannot remember. Nevertheless, with Grandma Lamb she did not seem to care who was around.

She not only walked around the house without a bra (brazier, as grandma would say). She was constantly walking around without panties. Doing either one did not make any sense to me at all. She could have taken her underwear and bra with her into the bathroom. She did not do that. I felt that actions speak louder than words. If she wanted us to be modest than she herself should show a little modesty. With kids, you should not have a double standard. It is either one way or the other. Kids mostly do as you do.

Remember that old admonishment "do as I say not as I do."

Naked In the Picture Window!!

Debbie was one of those kids who would not keep her clothes on. Every family has one. As soon as you would put Debbie's shoes, socks, and clothes on her, she would immediately take them off. As soon as Grandma Lamb or someone else got her dressed every morning, she took her clothes off. She was just that kind of a kid.

It was very frustrating to Grandma. She would get into one of her rages again and say, "By damned if you don't keep those clothes on I am going to beat the living daylights out of you". Debbie was a tiny little thing. She had sandy blonde hair. I always stood head and shoulders taller than she did. She had blue eyes. She was constantly in trouble for something or other.

Her constant side kick was Freddie. You rarely saw one of them that the other was not just around the corner.

She like me liked to suck on her two fingers. I sucked my forefinger and middle finger while Debbie sucked her middle two fingers. This was a sore spot for grandma too. She always seemed to do this and take her clothes off all at the same time.

None of it seemed to faze Debbie. The more you dressed Debbie the more she would take her clothes off. Grandma yelling at the top of her lungs did not enter into Debbie's consciousness. She seemed to be in a world all her own.

Grandma seemed to be at her wits end. She just did not seem to know what to do with her.

Grandma herself paraded and walked around naked. I guess since grandma walked around naked Debbie seemed to think it was ok for her to do it too. If this was, the case Grandma seemed to be oblivious of Debbie's plight. Grandma did not seem to understand the double standard. Grandma did not seem to think that she should set a good example. Setting a good example did not enter into grandma's vocabulary.

Well one-day grandma was at her wits end. She finally stripped Debbie naked herself. Then grandma proceeded to walk Debbie down the sidewalk stripped naked. Then she made Debbie stand on the porch stripped naked. If these things were not enough, she put Debbie in the picture window of our living room for about a half a day. Plastered her up there for all to see and made her stay there. Grandma would not let Debbie move one inch away from the window.

From this day forward, Debbie seemed to have nightmares about the living room picture window. Not only were her nightmares about the living room window. They were about people out to get her. Still other people were trying to chase her down.

Debbie became an introvert. She always thought people could not be trusted. She started talking to herself. Mumbling about how things would have or could have been different if mother was still alive. She was just basically talking to herself about everything and anything.

We never did talk about it. We all remembered it but we never talked about it. We were afraid the same thing would happen to any of the rest of us. So none of us went without clothes from that day forward it was a lesson we all seemed to learn. It was a quiet understanding.

We would pretend that if you did not talk about a certain thing maybe it really did not happen, that it only happened in our minds. We learned to ignore certain things. That what we saw did not really happen. Even if we did talk about it who would believe us anyway, we were just kids.

It would be our word against an adult.

Yes! The adult would lie about it and say they did not do that! On the other hand, they would say that we had done something to deserve it. Either way we would have been guilty of the crime committed.

We just could not believe our eyes that grandma had done such a horrible thing to one of us. Especially since her walking around naked all the time, seemed to us a far worse crime.

Grandma's Carpetbag Purse

Grandma's purses were unusually large bags, too big for her size. As a child they seemed bigger than grandma herself did. One might think she carried some of our stuff in there but she never did. She never carried anything in it except her wallet, her coin purse, and Kleenex tissues. She must have kept a whole box in this bag and in her pockets. You never wanted to use any of them though because you never knew which one would be a used Kleenex.

As if this was not bad enough when you went to the grocery store it was the pits. Here is this old woman pushing this cart with groceries around the store. Hanging on to her skirt strings were at least six little kids at any given time.

Her pockets were always bulging too, not because they were full of money by any stretch of the imagination but because they were always full of these

Kleenex. No these Kleenex were not clean either. Grandma was afraid to not keep her spare tissues around in every nook and cranny. She was afraid she would be caught unaware and need one for an emergency. Therefore, she kept all these Kleenex's for just such an emergency.

It was especially annoying during the checkout line at the grocery store. Grandma's coin purse was not the only place she kept loose coins. She kept coins in the bottom of this carpetbag, which was three times larger than it needed to be.

She also kept coins in every zippered compartment in the bag. Now that she is digging inside this bag for all the loose coins to finish, paying for her bill. The line behind her at the cash register is getting longer.

She has all these annoying little brats asking her all kinds of questions. They want gum or candy. She did not have the money to pay for these items. During the course of her search, she is starting to get annoyed and starts yelling for these kids to shut up.

During her search, however she unloads a boatload of Kleenex all over the counter top. The cashier asks grandma, "Mam, would you like me to throw those away." Grandma says, "No! I will keep them. I may need them." The longer grandma looks for some loose coins the more Kleenex comes out of her bag.

Now she starts digging through her pockets. Well there is Kleenex here too. While searching in her pockets she does manage to find a couple of pennies here too. The Kleenex from her pockets got put on the counter of the cash register. The whole time she is searching, she is counting out these much-needed coins.

Finally, after what seems like thirty minutes she has found enough coins to pay for the much-needed food items. Now begins the process of putting these Kleenex back into the storage unit they came from. She put these Kleenex back into her pockets. She put them back into her compartments in her bag. The rest of the Kleenex she stuffed back into the bottom of her carpetbag.

The most embarrassing time for me going to the grocery store was watching grandma go through all of these Kleenex just to get some groceries. The people behind us were starting to get annoyed too to say the least. I was always surprised no one ever said anything. They too may have been embarrassed.

Looking back, I laugh about it.

I too have Kleenex everywhere. I am trying to break this habit. Some habits you just do not want to keep. To this day, I occasionally dry a black pair of pants and find white lint all over them, from a forgotten Kleenex.

Mealtime

I have talked a lot about the many things that happened at our house but very little about the types of foods you would need to feed a family this size. How it worked sitting this many around the table at dinnertime.

I have not talked about sitting around the kitchen table. There were usually ten to thirteen people sitting around our table at any given time.

My favorite meal of the day was lunch. Every day we came home for lunch grandma would have us a hot meal ready and waiting for us. It was very good too.

It was mostly us younger ones and John and Larry that came home for lunch. There was also the ones not in school yet.

She had to peel about five pounds of potatoes to feed this group. Then she fried them until they were tender and golden brown. She added a batch of a dozen eggs in the midst of all of these potatoes. She beat the eggs until they were whipped and fluffy. She poured the eggs over the potatoes. She cooked this mixture until the eggs were not runny but soft. There was toast with melted butter. You could have jelly over the toast and it was the best meal you have ever eaten. The jelly was usually grandma's home-made jelly.

Another of my favorite meals was good old-fashioned navy bean soup. She would soak the beans overnight. Then early the next morning she would put them on to cook.

She always added ham hocks. They were cheaper than a ham and the skin around the ham hock made good broth for the bean soup. She added slivers of onions and carrots and cooked them right along with the beans. She simmered them all day long. When you came home from school and smelled the aroma of these beans, it made you hungry. Then she would cook some homemade corn bread to perfection and it was really sweet corn bread. Amazing what you can cook on a limited budget.

Cold cereal was expensive so we never had cold cereal it was a luxury. We did make toast in a bowl and when you are not used to eating cereal this was a real treat. Grandma did not seem to mind that we ate toast. She got us started. She let us toast the bread in the toaster. Then she taught us to break the bread into bite-sized pieces. We would then add sugar and milk it made the best cereal you have ever eaten.

The milk was whole, vitamin D, milk. We got two gallons of milk every other day to feed a family this large.

Chicken and noodles was another staple in our house. You could buy one chicken and it would make one great big pot of chicken stock, which made some great chicken and noodles. It usually had plenty of chicken chunks. We usually put some onions and carrots in the stockpot.

Another way to cook chicken was to make chicken and dumplings. Grandma taught to make some of the lightest fluffiest dumplings that melt in your mouth they were so light and fluffy. We added carrots and onions to this mixture as well. You could get by with just one chicken when you cooked food like this. Using all of the chicken including the skin, to make the broth made some good broth for both of these dishes.

We rarely had meat as a main dish at our house. We cooked the meat into a stew to make a main dish out of the meal.

When we all sat around the table there were eleven kids sitting around the table at one time. There were usually one or two kids in high chairs. There were usually two adults sitting with us.

It was not often that we all sat around the table together. Dad's business was such that he worked late at night. When we got home from school, he was at the garage. Junior, Larry, and John usually went straight to the garage after school. They were not sitting around the table during the week. On weekends and for breakfast they were home and eating at the table. Dad made benches that went the whole length of both sides of the table. This provided more seating spaces. There were not enough chairs for all to have a chair of their own.

The bigger kids sat on the end and made the younger kids sit in the middle of the bench. One bench was up against the wall. There was no space between the wall and the first bench. When you sat there, you were stuck until the meal was over. The seating arrangement did not give you much space.

We did not pass the food as most people do. We put the food on the table, and then we just grabbed the food. First come first served. You did not know if there was ever going to be enough food to go around. If you did not grab fast you did not get a choice piece.

On Sundays, we sometimes had meat for the main meal. It was at times like these when you noticed the choicest pieces of chicken going first. The back, neck, and wings were left overs.

We had mashed potatoes and gravy with a side of another vegetable. Sometimes we even got to have homemade pies. Sunday dinners were usually the best meal of the week. Dad was home and he wanted it this way.

Grandma's Favorites

Grandma had her favorites. I was not one of grandma's favorites. There was Daryl. He had sandy colored hair. He was fair skinned and smiled all the time. Grandma called him her little boy blue. He had blue eyes. He was a very sweet natured boy. Everyone loved Daryl. He loved everybody too. He was the baby of the family. He did not get to know our mother like most of the rest of us did. He was only eight months old when she died. Everyone protected him. We took turns protecting him from the bullies at school. We also protected him from the bullies at home.

Daryl could hear and play music in his head. At a very early age, he could hear a song on the radio and be able to play it on the piano. He was that good. It is just too bad this could not have been channeled into something more. He was a natural musician.

Vera was also another one of grandma's favorite. She played dad's violin and she would not let any of the rest of us touch it. Vera was the oldest girl. She had blue eyes and was never very happy. However, she and grandma were always close because grandma was with her at infancy during the war. Vera was a lot like grandma.

Then there was the one who was always playing pranks on people, that was John. John's pranks bordered on bullying. He had an ornery streak, which bordered on meanness. He had sandy blonde hair. He was the family bully and the class bully.

Then there were all the rest of us. We seemed to be in the way. It seemed like she hated the very ground I walked on. I was not the only one she hated though.

She hated Freddie and Debbie too at least the three of us could not seem to do anything right in her eyes. It took a while, but her true colors showed up eventually. Yes, we learned in order to keep peace we had to keep out of grandma's way. Oh! Not all of us just the ones she could not stand to even look at.

Her favorites did not have to stay out of her way. John, Vera and lastly and most favored of all was Daryl. Vera and Daryl were favored because she was around them both from infancy. John was a different case all together. She loved his antics and she would tell of his escapades repeatedly. The time she loved most was when John was younger and he knocked dad out with a brick. She told them with relish and with glee. Grandma treated us all differently and some of us unfairly.

It took quite a while for the stupor that we had all been in since mother's death to wear off. It seems harder to lose a loved one at such an early age maybe because we do not understand. We were all living in a kind of haze even Grandma Lamb. Then to wake up from this haze to see and feel the tortures that Grandma Lamb was putting us through. We just could not believe our eyes.

When mother was alive, Grandma seemed nice now she was being mean just like dad. We did not see much of him in the beginning. He would work and work and did not drink for a while. Dad's not drinking did not last all that long. I think dad quit drinking for less than two months. Therefore, instead of dad being the bad person all the time, Grandma took over the abuses, at least at home.

For Debbie, Freddie and me it was hard to be around Grandma. She beat us at every turn. We did not go into the living room or any other room of the house, if grandma was there, she terrified us that much.

Grandma had a habit of grabbing our hair by the ponytail. It hurt a lot. Then she would grab our hair and just start yanking. You did not even have to be doing anything wrong. She did it just in case you were thinking of doing something wrong to remind you. You would try to sneak past her and she would grab your hair and pull you back to where she was standing.

Debbie has sandy hair and blue eyes. She always had a terrified look on her face. Debbie and Freddie both were skittish like I was. They too were gullible like I was. I do not know what made us like that, except for maybe no protection from the two bully's in the family. Perhaps the entire trauma in our lives made us skittish and fearful. We could not seem to shake the fearful attitude that would control of our emotions. Debbie seemed to be the worst to have this fearful attitude.

Back Country Drives

Grandma did give us some good moments. She was not always mean to us kids. I remember her taking us for afternoon drives in the summertime. Most of the time, we visited her daughter our Aunt in Springfield, Ohio. Our Aunt had five kids of her own.

Sometimes we would go to our great Aunt's farm in Mount Sterling, Ohio. Here they allowed us to feed the goats. We fed the sheep. We ran around the farm to our hearts content. We made a lot of noise. Then we would chase the chickens, it was great fun. Of course, if you have ever had chickens you know this is a big No! No! We got into trouble for this. After a while, I think they hated seeing us come because of our chicken chasing.

Two things they had were impressive. They still had a pump for their water outside. They still had an outhouse. They were poor and indoor plumbing was very expensive. We were city slickers and had never been without indoor plumbing. Therefore, it was a real novelty to have to go to the bathroom outside.

Occasionally she would take us other places.

She would take us to places where she used to play when she was growing up. Like the old Jonathan Alder's homestead. She showed us the one room schoolhouse where she used to go as a little girl. We would walk around and explore. We used to peek into the window to see where the desk would sit. It seemed so different to today's classrooms. Grandma Lamb said she only went through school to the eighth grade.

She would show us the gravesites of her parents. She would regale us with stories of our great grandparents. In addition, our great-great grandparent's graves were here. A lot of the Morgan's before her had gravesites here as well. She would tell of her (our) ancestry. Of course, we never knew them but she would tell us stories about them anyway.

Sometimes we could get her off on a tangent and she would talk about it a long time. She used to say, "My dad was something really special. (You could see she really loved her dad. Her eyes would light up with a sparkle and a smile.) He used to take us on horse and buggy rides on a Sunday afternoons. In the winter he would change the buggy into a sleigh."

These were fun times. It was hard not see the picture of a carriage being made into a sleigh. It did sound like a lot of fun. Sometimes on the way back home, she would stop in West Jefferson and get all of us an ice-cream cone. For a family as large and poor as ours an ice-cream cone was a real treat.

I did not realize it then, that these would be some of my most cherished memories as a child, the stories of family history that I could write about later on. It made the hot summer days tolerable.

However treasured, these memories were to us we never gave it a thought until as adults we realized, our older brothers did not get to go on these outings. They were always too busy working at the garage. They never heard these stories. They never saw grandma come to life just remembering her father. We all got the impression that she was her father's favorite.

The older boys never saw the old homestead. They did not get to go to our aunt's house very often. They did not get to go and play on the farm. Dad always had them working down at the garage. They did not get to play with the cousins. They did not get to pick an ear of corn at least, not at this time. They did not get to pet the animals because these were grandma's and mother's relatives. They were always with dad.

I loved these times best of all learning all the family history and hearing Grandma's old stories. It was times like these when I knew I had to be a writer to tell all these stories to everyone else.

I think Grandma Lamb wanted us to learn these stories so that we could tell her great-grandchildren. She did not want us to forget our stories.

She told us these stories repeatedly. Grandma wanted to make sure we would remember them. All the girls remember them the boys not so much.

Larry said, "I never once got to go on those rides with grandma."

Christmas When I was Eight

Dad's favorite time of year was still the Christmas Holidays. Christmas was the only time of the year he was consistent. He was like a little boy all over again. Nothing seemed to bother him at Christmas. He still spent the week between Christmas and the New Year sober. Every year it was the same and had been for as long as I could remember. It seemed like he was trying to make up for everything that had gone wrong all year.

If he did drink during this time, he never let us see him drink. He never had beer in the house during Christmas and New Year.

He started on Christmas Eve getting six of the scrawniest, ugliest trees on the lot. We were very poor, and usually on Christmas Eve, they were free or next to nothing. That was not the only reason for decorating on Christmas Eve though. This was a tradition his grandfather had brought over from Germany that his parents taught him. The Christmas tree would be up until Epiphany sometime in January.

Dad would take these four or five scrawny little trees. He would take his pocketknife; string; wire; and a drill. He would build one of the most beautiful trees you have ever laid your eyes on. He would drill a hole here and put in a branch there. He would do the same all over the tree until it looked magnificent. It usually took dad several hours to prepare his creation. However, he was in his element and he loved every minute of it.

Dad had built a table for the Christmas tree long before I was born. When the tree was ready dad set it into its stand. Dad built this table and mounted the tree stand into the center. Also on this table dad had mounted a train track. When our Christmas tree had all the extra branches, it needed Dad put the tree in the tree stand. Then the tree was ready for the decorations.

The older kids helped while the not so older kids, middle-aged kids watched the younger ones. There were too many kids for all to decorate at once so they had a good system set up for this special event.

One had to earn the right to decorate by age only. As one got older, it was their turn either to watch the younger ones or to decorate. Too many hands would have made a mess. Nevertheless, the not so older kids did not really mind because they knew their turn was coming. They knew they would be an older kid and we could not wait.

We also read stories to the younger kids. Their favorite two stories were 'Twas the Night before Christmas' and 'The Littlest Angel.' We would finally get them off to sleep or at least most of them off to sleep.

Then we said, "Now you have to be quiet. We will sneak down and see what it is like, then come back up and tell you all about it." Well the younger ones thought it was a grand idea. They had to promise not to follow and not to make a sound. The not so older ones taught the younger ones how to do it. It was a tradition for us to do it again this year.

We would sneak down and watch as the magic transformed our living room. This year it was John's and my turn to creep down the steps to watch the process. I remember when Larry and Karen would sneak down and then come up and tell us.

I did not like having to wait my turn. Nor did Debbie like having to wait her turn this year. She gave John and me a fit about it. We had to make sure she would not wake the others up before we could leave.

I do not know if our parents knew this part of the tradition but it was another story we kids never told.

Wow! What a process it was too! Dad would take the lights out of their boxes and put them around the tree. The garland came next. The ornaments and bulbs were next. Dad always called them toys, jewels, and trinkets.

Every toy placed on the tree was magical. The little horns actually blew a sound. The birds had real feathers. The man on the rocking horse was not glued on he had movable arms and legs. The toy soldier's arms and legs actually moved.

As we watched, the very air seemed to take on a magical spell. John's eyes were as big as saucers as mine must have been, just from watching. We could not wait until the magical age of helping. We knew it could not be long. We were already the not so older ones.

After the toys, trinkets, and glass bulbs, came the final touch the icicles, many icicles. Dad loved icicles (tinsel) he loved the way the slightest breeze would make it move around and sparkle with the lights. We too loved the way the icicles moved when a slight breeze would hit it. Sometimes we would purposely blow on them to make them move and watch the sparkle.

Then the lights went off. The tree lights turned on just to see their handy work. Oh! Every year I think it was more beautiful than the year before. The different colored lights shimmered and bounced off the wall and on the floor and everywhere, where it hit the icicles.

Then dad would take some cotton full of sparkles and place it on top of the table. We would pretend it was snow for the village. Then very carefully, he would place the village around the tree. The barber shop here, the country store there, a tree here, a man there and of course a snowman or two. Our Christmas tree never had to worry about being lonely even if we were all in bed. It had many things to keep it company. We had a full-fledged village under there.

Then the tin train on the tracks came next. The whistle would blow, the smoke stack actually smoked and light on the front of the engine would light up. The train would run merrily and happily around the tree and village, as if it did not have a care in the world.

Then dad would take painted cardboard and wrap it around the table. This cardboard looked like bricks around a chimney. Then he would hang our stockings on the edge of the table. Dad always made sure before we went to bed, that we left a sock for Santa.

Dad would say, "It does not matter if I cannot tell them apart because Santa can tell them apart." What a clever man he was sometimes. You forgot what had transpired throughout the year. Christmas was still the best time.

Next came the present wrapping. We all usually got one or two presents. The girls always got a doll. The boys always got either a truck or car for Christmas. Now however, John and I would creep back up the steps to let the others know what had transpired around the tree.

It would still be a while before we would be allowed to unwrap the presents though. After we told the younger ones of all the sights, we had seen we had to insist they go to sleep or Santa would not come. This seemed to satisfy most of them.

There were still those who were just about ready to quit believing. But those doubters were not quite sure.

If there was snow like there sometimes was, someone would go out on the roof near one of the bedroom windows and put sleigh tracks, and hoof prints of eight tiny reindeer.

Then somewhere around four or five o'clock in the morning someone from down stairs would bellow "HO! HO! HO!" until we were all awake. Even if some of us were faking it, we never let on. It was part of the magic. They wanted us to think Santa had said, "HO! HO! HO!" We believed.

By the time, we got downstairs Santa had disappeared. His reindeer's tracks were on the roof where someone

had put them. How could you not believe
when the air still held the magic?

We would all go see the train and
the village. Then the delight of watching
the presents unwrapped was every bit as
much fun as watching our dad decorate
the tree.

The Liar

One day on my way to school I dawdled! I was slow. I was looking at everything along the way. All of my older brothers and sisters had run on ahead of me. I only had Larry and John. Junior, Vera, and Karen had moved on to Junior High school or high school. John and Larry did not want their bratty little sister seen with them. I was not that crazy about school anyway just something I had to do.

I was left on my own to get to school on time. They would not wait for me to catch up with them. When I dawdled it made me late for school. I was in Big Time Trouble! I got called to the principal's office.

The Principal wanted to know why I was late. I had no idea. I did not know that I had dawdled. I was scared waiting on the principal to come to her office. No kid wants to admit they did anything wrong. Then you know for sure you are in trouble. I kept thinking I had to go to the Principal's office. This is scary stuff.

The principal asked, "Why are you late?"

I said, "I don't know."

The principal smacked me on the face and said, "Yes, you do too know why you are late! Why are you late? Do not lie to me."

Again I said, "I do not know." The principle again smacked me on the face because she thought I was lying. Just like grandma would do.

The principle asked me again, "Why are you late?"

I had to come up with something because the next step to being smacked at our house was getting a beating I said, "I was late because my grandma stayed up late to watch the news and didn't get up to get me to school." I thought to myself that sounded pretty good she ought to believe this. That gets me off the hook. I could not tell her I had dawdled that would only get me into more trouble.

The principal said, "Well than I will just call your Grandma and we will get to the bottom of this."

I thought to myself Oh! Now I am really in trouble with a capital T. Grandma will beat me for sure. I started crying. I did not know what to do now. Grandma already hated me. I did not need the principle calling her on the phone, for grandma to come to the school. Grandma hated the phone. She hated being called down to the principal's office for one of her grandchildren even more. I knew I was in major trouble now.

Grandma Lamb came to the school. The principal asked her what time she went to bed. The principal told grandma she needed to get to bed on time; so that she could get up on time; to get the kids to school on time. The principal said, "Norma told me that you were up late watching the news. You could not get out of bed to get her to school on time."

Grandma said, "Well that little liar. I had to work. When I got home, I watched the news until I went to bed. She is telling you a lie."

Well grandma took me home. The principal let grandma take me home.

Just outside of the exit were some evergreen bushes. Grandma broke off a great big branch, well not too big. It was big enough to make a good switch. She took this branch and hit me all the way home. It stung too. It stung my legs. It stung my back, my arms, my head and anything that it hit on my body. It left a big welt wherever it hit.

I was embarrassed all the kids in the school was peeking out the window and laughing at me. I was humiliated. I never dawdled again after that. I was always on time.

All the way home while grandma was hitting me she said, "You little liar! You are nothing but a liar! You little liar! You are nothing but a liar! You little liar! By damned you had better not tell another lie about me at that school you little liar!"

You would have thought that would have been the end of it but it was not.

Every time after this incident I was classified as a liar. I could not open my mouth and speak. Every time I spoke the truth grandma called me a liar. If I told a lie, she believed me. I got confused when I spoke the truth I was a liar. When I lied I was telling the truth.

It got me to the point where it did not matter what I said. Even I did not know the truth anymore. I myself could not keep it straight. Every chance grandma got she called me a liar. It seemed like she would create things to make me answer questions so that she had an excuse to call me a liar.

All my brothers and sisters called me a liar as well! You see in our house, if one person is being picked on the rest were left alone. So this is the way it was. I was the house liar.

"Liar! Liar! Pants on fire!"

"Liar! Liar! Pants on fire!"

On and on it went. Nothing I could do about it. Grandma Lamb would just laugh and laugh. She would not say anything to anyone about it. She too called me a liar.

I had two nicknames. My other nickname was crybaby.

I was not the only one with a nickname. Debbie's nickname was dumbdumb Debbie. Fred's nickname was Freddie the freeloader.

Karen's nicknames were big foot and doofus. Dad and grandma called us these ridiculous names to make us feel bad about ourselves and they stuck. Everyone called us these names. We could never redeem ourselves. It seemed like no one else got a nickname.

Even as an adult, I still do not like nicknames.

Grandma and Dad's Relationship

Grandma's and Dad's relationship still was not the greatest. They learned to tolerate each other if not respect, each other a little. They were both hot heads.

Neither dad nor grandma would back down from a fight. Grandma was smaller. She learned Dad was bigger. Both were ornery old goats. Grandma knew she was always going to lose so she became the first to back down. Grandma was four feet nine inches tall. Dripping wet she weighed ninety-eight pounds.

She always said, "I might be small but I am mighty."

While Dad was five feet ten and a half inches tall. He weighed around one hundred and ninety pounds.

There was one time in particular when grandma did not back down from the fight. She hit dad on the head with an iron skillet. Dad went down in a flash on the kitchen floor. Grandma thought for sure that she was a goner this time. It must have sobered them both up. When dad woke up neither one of them had the urge to fight for the rest of that night. Dad looked at grandma with a little more respect in his eyes.

Later he told the story with relish. He even added a few of his own embellishments to the story to make it lively. He wanted to make grandma look feistier than she was. She was feisty.

One other time they were fighting and grandma picked up a butcher knife. Once she thought of it, she laid the knife back down on the table. I think she knew she would never get by with it since dad had twice the strength and twice the size. They still argued but they never had any more fights. I think they were afraid someone could get hurt.

They did continue to fight a lot, mostly arguing that is. It seemed that they both almost relished the idea of a good fight. Dad was glad Grandma was there. He also knew that grandma blamed him for killing her daughter.

It took a while but eventually they learned where to draw the line. Each knew the other one wanted only the best for the kids. Even if they could not agree or went about it in different ways as to how to help us kids. They were doing it for Ella, our mother.

Grandma was too proud to ask Dad for a dime to run the household. If she needed money to buy groceries, she earned it herself. Dad did give her a little for things like bread and milk but it was not nearly enough to feed eleven growing kids and two adults on.

Sometimes our brother Jr. would sneak around and get grandma some money out of dad's wallet. He was usually so drunk he never knew how much money he had. He never missed a cent of it. Now grandma on the other hand knew exactly every cent she had in her billfold. If someone took it out of her billfold, she knew that too.

Little brothers and sisters only do what bigger brothers and sisters do. If they see them taking (stealing) money out of dads or grandma's wallet or billfold they are going to do it too.

There was a time when dad and his younger brother were painting our house. They had been at it for quite a while. My uncle Bob had been a good influence on my dad. He actually managed to make my dad stay sober for a while.

My uncle and my dad cooked up this scheme to tease grandma. Everyone knew the strongest coffee in the world was grandma's coffee. She used to make a pot of coffee in the morning leaving it boiling all day long, on top of the gas stove. The grounds would still be in the basket. She still drank it. She expected everyone else to do as she did. She felt the longer it cooked the better it was. She felt what was good enough for her was good enough for everyone.

This time Uncle Bob said, "Grandma your coffee is so strong it can make a fork stand straight up, see, look!"

Grandma said, "Oh my goodness! That is strong coffee."

She did not know they had put an apple in the bottom of the cup. As Uncle Bob pulled the fork out, out came the apple. Grandma started laughing. She did not laugh very often. She loved teasing. Dad and Uncle Bob were the jokesters. It was even harder to pull the wool over grandma's eyes. She enjoyed a good joke and our dad was good at that.

Dad and Uncle Bob made a good team. Uncle Bob's job was installing elevators. He was very good at his job.

Grandpa Baas taught all his boys (our dad and uncles) to be very meticulous at anything they did.

Grandpa taught them to sand wood down to be as smooth as a baby's butt.

Saturday Night Donuts

Saturday night was donut night. Usually Grandma Lamb made the donuts. If she did not feel up to making the donuts, there was a donut shop just around the corner, from our house. She would send someone out for a dozen. A baker's dozen was exactly enough to feed all of us. We always got glazed donuts. Glazed seemed to be everyone's favorite and it was cheaper. There was no fighting, who would get what donut we all got the same.

It was fun and they tasted very good. It was a rarity for us to get store bought items, especially donuts, these were a luxury not a necessity. To get store bought donuts was the best. The donuts Grandma made were very good. It was just more fun to have store bought.

To watch her go about sifting all the flour; adding the sugar; getting the lard just hot enough for deep-frying. It was a long drawn out process but it was well worth the wait and you usually got more than one with the homemade donuts. It was also a real special treat to get a store bought donut. We all loved them both equally.

Now if grandma forgot what day it was we would send Daryl to remind grandma. She very obligingly said, "Oh so it is," and immediately, she would send someone to the store, or she would get us busy helping her make donuts.

On these nights, you could almost forget the bad things that had happened and would probably happen again tomorrow. For tonight when we were eating the donuts, savoring the flavor, and smell these delicious delights. We could pretend that the other life did not exist if only for a moment.

We always sent Daryl to ask grandma (poor thing) because grandma was never ever mad or angry with him. She bullied and terrified most of the rest of us. Grandma worshiped the ground

Daryl walked on. He could do no wrong. He was her little boy blue.

There were times when we would forget ourselves. One of us other than Daryl would remind grandma it was donut night. Grandma would have a conniption fit because we tried this. Grandma said, "If I wanted to buy donuts I do not need you to tell me to buy them. What do you think money grows on trees? Well money does not grow on trees so don't ask again!" On those nights there were not any donuts. Grandma had worked herself up so bad you would think she was having a heart attack.

Daryl became our go between or liaison between grandma and us. He did not mind. He loved grandma. It was a mutual admiration society. He probably felt a little superior about it but if he did, he never let on. He was just a happy go lucky kind of a kid. He was the baby of the family that always had a ready smile on his face. Daryl always wanted to please everyone and get along with everyone. Everyone loved him for it.

My Recurring Nightmare

My recurring nightmare at this time is my Mother lying there in the casket. She is dead. She is cold and she is hard. My Mother is not soft anymore. I wanted my soft mother. The person I could talk to no matter what.

"Aaaahhh!" She is so cold and hard. It scared me to feel this hard, cold thing that looks like my mother. My mother is not hard and cold she is soft and warm. I want my mother. I want my mother, to get up and take me home. "Aaaahhh!" I am six years old. No one had told me she was even sick. No one said she was dying. No one has told me she was dead. "Aaaahhh!" I am screaming and crying hysterically. Someone smacks me to get my attention. It does not work. I am still screaming harder than before. I am totally out of control. I hear them say, "We have got to get her out of here, she is making a scene." No one tries to comfort me.

I finally realize it is my other grandmother. It is Grandma Baas, the scary one. The grandma that does not like us very much, she grabbed a hold of my arm and started pulling and tugging on me. She had someone take me out of the Funeral Home without telling me anything; without comforting me. She is the one who is smacking me.

I am getting on everyone's nerves. I know I am but I cannot seem to help it. I just cannot seem to quit crying. I am hysterical. I do not understand. No one is talking to me. None of my older brothers and sisters is even here, just all those grown-ups I do not know.

"Hick-up, hick-up, hick-up," I am so tired and so drained the crying has almost stopped, but not quite. I almost have it under control. I am desperately trying to quit crying. They keep hitting me and hitting me to make me quit crying. It is not working. It just seems to make me cry more. It just makes me more hysterical.

"Stop that this instant, stop that infernal hick-upping and crying or I will make you wish you had quit." I do not even remember who was talking.

"She is the oldest of the six younger ones."

"We would not want the rest of those kids making another scene. A scene like this one is making with their mother like this. Keep the rest of them out of here. Do not let any of the other younger ones come in here to see their mother. Especially since she had such a strong reaction they were meaning me."

I want to know what they are talking about, but I was a quiet child. I did not ask questions, I was too afraid to ask. I do not know most of these people.

I would wake up in a cold sweat chilled to the bone. Night after night, I had this nightmare of a dream. To me it was a nightmare never knowing where I was or where my Mother was.

I wanted my Mother back. I wanted her to come home. I prayed to God that He would bring her back to life, as He did His Son Jesus. He never did. Finally, I quit praying about it. I quit asking God to bring her back to life. It was not going to work with my Mother.

My dreams were scrambled and disjointed with missing pieces and missing facts. They seemed scary and real as if I was reliving it again and again. It was not fun. I hated these nightmarish dreams

.

The Tom Boy Wanna Be

When I was eight years old, I wanted to be just like my older sister Karen. She was a tomboy. All the boys liked Karen. She played baseball better than the boys did. She played basketball better than the boys did. She even played football better than the boys did. She loved sports. She also loved it that she played better than the boys did. She loved it that the boys all wanted her on their team too because she played that well.

In order for me to be like her, I had to practice things like climbing trees. I thought this would make me look less like a sissy. I was always in the house taking care of the kids and helping to clean the house. I had always helped mother do these things. It was just natural for me to continue to do these things. There were five brothers and sisters younger than me who still needed help. I was just beginning to like boys. All the boys I liked preferred Karen best. I did not have time to learn how to play sports. This summer I was going to learn how to do all these things.

I started by following Larry and John two of my older brothers everywhere. Whenever they were home which was not very often, I went where they went. Of course, they still considered me a little kid. John was nine and Larry was not eleven yet. I was eight. I could not understand why they did not want me to tag along, so I did it anyway. I just did not let them know I was following them everywhere. I would show up in the least likely places.

John did not mind nearly as much as Larry did. John liked being somebodies hero. He liked having a tag-a-long.

The first thing John was going to teach me was how to jump off a roof, land in a tree, and climb down the tree. Instead of just climbing the tree, I was to jump off the roof first. I was very excited about learning something new. Larry did not think that John should teach me anything though. He still thought of me as the little sister, an annoyance. Larry thought of me as a baby and his bratty little sister but I was not a baby. I argued that I was taller than both of them were but that did not matter to Larry. Age was what mattered to him. John liked people to be daring and that is what I wanted to be. I wanted to do something daring.

Larry disappeared and John was the only one left to teach me. If the game, was not daring enough John made it more daring. John said, "All you have to do is follow me. Do what I do. Follow me exactly." John jumped from the roof to the tree. Then he climbed down to the ground. It was a very large Maple tree. It had many leaves and many branches everywhere. It was a huge tree, how could I miss. I hated heights. I was not going to let John call me a sissy any more. This scared me though. I was very determined to jump. I was very excited and very scared about jumping from the roof to the tree.

John said, "One, two, three jump!"
I stood there on the roof rooted to the
spot. I tried to jump nothing happened. It
was as if my feet were lead weight. I had
never done anything so daring. I was the
house bound mouse. I was always working in the house. I was always taking care
of everyone. I took care of the ones
younger than me. There were still five
brothers and sisters younger for me to
care for. For me to do something so
daring so scary and frightening I just
could not do it. I was completely and
utterly terrified of getting hurt. I had a
very low tolerance for being bad. This I
knew this was going to be very, very bad.

John said it again, "Ready set one,
two, three jump." John was getting very
impatient with me now. He said, "Yep
just like I thought you are a sissy just like
all the other girls around here. You don't
want to be a tom-boy like Karen." I said,
"I do too. I can do it. It just takes me
longer." I could not tell John I was
scared. Then he would know for sure that
I was a sissy. John said, "I am only going
to give you one more chance and then I

am done with it. You can figure out another way to become a tom-boy and I will not help you anymore."

John said, "Ready set go." I did go too finally. I jumped. Whew! I was flying in the air. I was thinking, Wee this is fun! I closed my eyes. I did not want to see what I was doing. I tried to grab the tree branch but with my eyes closed, I missed. Ouch! Ouch! I started screaming at the top of my lungs. I was screaming and crying all at the same time! "Help, Aaaggghhh! Help me!" It seemed like hours before help came. When you have so many kids, someone is always screaming like they are hurt.

I was stuck on the fence post. I landed smack dab on the pointed edge of the gatepost. It had a point on the tip. This post tip was inside of me. I could not get off. The pain from this made me paralyzed. It was approximately four inches in diameter and about six inches long. I was stuck. It was inside of me between my legs. I am still screaming. I cannot move I am too numb to move. It hurt so badly. It was the most excruciating pain I had ever felt.

John took off. He was nowhere to be found. He did not try to help me. He just disappeared. I suppose he felt guilty. John did not get me any help either. Maybe he was afraid I would tell everyone he had caused it. Maybe he was afraid he would get the blame.

Maybe if I had opened my eyes to see where I was going this would not have happened. I did close my eyes. It did happen.

Finally, help arrives. Grandma Lamb and one of my aunts had come to rescue me from the fence post. It took both of them to lift me off the gatepost. I was stuck that severely. However, they did manage to lift me off.

They carried me to the couch in the living room. They put a blanket and towels under me. I was bleeding. I was still screaming and crying. Tears were rolling down my face. Grandma kept hollering at me to shut up and be quiet.

There is nothing to keep you crying this much. However, I just could not quit crying. It hurt too badly to quit. Then there was all the blood that did not seem to want to quit. I thought I was going to die no one told me otherwise.

Not once did anyone try to comfort me. All my brothers and sisters who were home at the time wanted to know why I was screaming. My aunt's kids must have been there too. My aunt usually came with her kids, our cousins.

No one came into the living room. The other kids had been told, "Leave the living room, and do not come back until it was ok". Ok for whom I wanted to ask. No one once told me I was not going to die. I was bleeding so badly and the pain was so severe. No one held me. No one rocked me. Of course maybe I was too big to be rocked.

My grandmother and my aunt just watched me bleed. I did not understand what was so fascinating about watching someone bleed. I did not understand a grandma or an aunt not wanting to help or to give comfort. It was times like these that I really missed my mother. It felt as if I was dying.

Was I being a crybaby? I did not think so. The pain was excruciating. It felt like someone had taken a knife to my insides. They did not ask me how I felt. I felt like my insides were on fire. I felt like I was going to be just like my mother, dead. I did not die. I just felt like I was going to die. I prayed that I would die. I wanted to die.

They never took me to the doctors to see if I was okay. They did not take me to the doctors to see if there was any internal damage done. Grandma and my Aunt just stood there and watched me bleed.

If this was not enough pain and problems, it seemed every month after this incident happened I had cramps. The cramps were so bad they were unbearable. I screamed and cried. Every month it was the same thing. Grandma Lamb told me to, "Shut-up and be quiet. I cannot take any more of your infernal crying. You will go to school."

I was not able to help myself. My body seemed to be in control of me. I did not have any control of the pain. The severe cramping just would not go away.

It hurt so badly I usually missed school for about two days. Every month because I was in so much pain it was the same thing. It felt like my insides were going to bust open and start bleeding again. I would start cramping all over again. It was the same pain as when I fell out of the tree. Oh! How grandma hated me for this.

I do not know if my body just wanted me to remember what had happened. This pain seemed to be as bad, if not worse than when I fell out of that tree. There seemed to be no apparent reason, at least not any visible sign, to explain my cramping.

I found out years later that when a young girl's body goes through a trauma like this it wants to start the cycle of her monthly periods. I did not start my monthly cycles until about four years later when I was twelve.

It seemed like my body was rejecting whatever had happened. My body did not like it one bit. I did not like it either.

I wished I could die. It hurt that badly.

Grandma Lamb from this day forward called me a crybaby. Then everyone else in the family did the same. Once you got a nickname, it was with you for the rest of your life.

Being a crybaby was worse than being a sissy. They already called me a liar, now I was a crybaby too. I was a lying, crybaby sissy. It was worse than Deb biscuit eater was. It was worse than big foot and clumsy. I would much rather be called a sissy anyway.

I never became a tomboy. John quit the "exercises". I was a lying, crybaby sissy. Believe me if I could have stopped crying I would have stopped crying. The cramping just would not go away.

When I became an adult the doctors told me I had severe scar tissue in my vaginal area and I was lucky I had one child. There would be no more children.

What Makes You Special?

What makes you think you are special?

The one thing that could have made me special did not make me special. Because whenever anyone called attention to this, my older sister would pull me aside and say, "They think you look like our mother but I lived with her. I know you do not look a thing like mother. They are wrong! Karen is the meek one, the loving one like our mother, not you."

Well this hurt. Every time someone called attention to this, Vera had something mean and nasty to say to me to make me feel bad and inferior. This made her feel superior to us to knock each one of us down a peg or two. It seemed like she looked for ways to knock us down a peg or two.

I did not realize it but what they saw in me was a resemblance of my mother at the age I currently was. Not the age of an adult when we knew her. I would get out one of my mother's pictures and not see any resemblance either. Oh! Maybe a little bit around the eyes. It must have been there because they always knew who I was and called me by name. Actually, they did not know my name. They always said, "Oh! You must be Ellree's daughter; you look so much like her." I did not have a name. Ellree was the nickname that someone with a close family connection would call our mother. Her real name was Ella Loree.

Vera's resentment of us grew as we grew older. One day Debbie was a spoiled brat all day long. She acted up at every turn. She would not do anything Vera told her to do. Vera finally whipped Debbie with a hairbrush. I was too terrified, not to do as I was told. I did not like Vera's 'threats' just threatening me was enough.

I unobtrusively as always hid in the background so that Vera would not notice me ever. I stayed hidden away, doing only what Vera said. I stayed out of her way.

She dressed Debbie up like a doll. She took her to the corner drugstore for an ice-cream cone. I did not know this until Vera came home bragging about it. Telling me, I was not going to get anything. I did not get any. I was hurt over this. It really showed me how much people cared. I was the good kid and got nothing. Debbie was the bad kid and got an ice-cream cone.

Perhaps Vera felt guilty for whipping Debbie but still it hurt. It seemed in Vera's eyes I could do nothing right. Everyone catered to Debbie because of her size. Even I too catered to Debbie. I would try to teach her things but she would say, "I can't! I am too little. I don't want to." It was always easier for me to do it myself then to try to teach her. I compensated for her lack out of frustration. I ended up always doing my chores and her chores to keep her from getting a whipping. I did this out of habit from watching my older brothers and sisters.

Now Debbie's frustration stems from being my little sister. Her size gave her trouble doing things like washing dishes and using the vacuum sweeper. She would get frustrated and quit trying. Debbie would watch me and see that I was capable of the most menial tasks. I was twice her size even though we were only eighteen months apart. Oh! What frustration she went through trying to be just like me. She was jealous of me because I could do everything so well, even the first time through.

We did not find these things out until very much later when we were adults and had children of our own. We never knew both of us were jealous of the other. We never tried to undermine the other though, not yet anyway.

I know I was not the only one Vera bullied. There was a time that Karen worked hard all day long for the neighbor. This neighbor had Karen do yard work all the time for her. This time in particular she had Karen cut the grass, do the trimming, and the edging. For all her hard work, Karen got a crinoline. We were poor and these things were a luxury. Crinolines were in style. Karen's was a beautiful creation, lacy and full. It made her full skirts flare out beautifully.

Vera was jealous. Grandma Lamb had bought Vera one but it was not as beautiful. After Vera saw Karen's, Vera's was not good enough anymore. Vera took Karen's crinoline, put on her high heels, and stomped on it until it was completely ruined.

Karen got into trouble for her crinoline being destroyed. Grandma thought Karen had been disrespectful of something so beautiful. It was not her fault. Vera just could not stand any of us having something nice.

Joan was always special because she was one of the twins. She hated being called a twin. No one ever knew her name. They would just say, "Oh! You must be one of the twins." "You don't look a thing like your twin brother." It was a back handed compliment. Then they would say, "How come he is so tall and you are so small?" Joan would just meekly say, "I don't know." How was she to know? Then they would say things like, "Freddie and Debbie look more like twins than you and Jimmy." What do you say to that? What could have made them special did not because everyone made it seem like a curse. So it really did not make them special either, just resentful.

Junior was the oldest boy, which made him special and our dad's right hand man.

Vera was the oldest girl.

Karen was the first child born after the war. Our parents love child.

Larry was first boy born after the war. This in itself made Larry special.

John was the ornery boy with lots and lots of personality and escapades to brag about.

Then there was me (Norma Jean) who observed and stayed in the back-ground. I did not want to make waves. It was safer for me to stay in the background and have no one notice me or so I thought.

Debbie was tiny and used her size to get people to feel sorry for her and to have people do things for her.

Freddie was one of our mother's favorite boys. She thought he was the most beautiful baby. He is one of the few of us who had a baby portrait made. Vera Junior and the twins were the only others with baby pictures.

The twins Jimmy was born five minutes before his twin sister Joan. He had dark almost black hair and brown eyes just like our mother. He was always happy and smiling too.

Joan was Jimmy's twin sister. She had blue eyes and sandy colored hair which grew darker as she got older.

Daryl was the baby. Everyone protected Daryl. He was everyone's favorite. He never knew our mother. He was grandma's little boy blue.

It seemed no matter what we did we were always lumped together. No one outside of our immediate family ever called us anything but the Baas children. Even though three, four or more families had the name, Baas. They always called us, 'The Baas Children'.

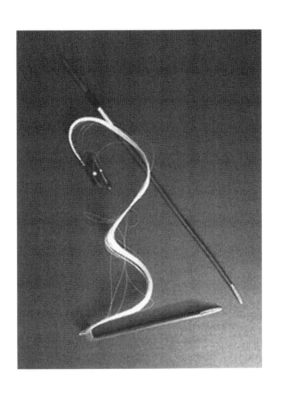

The Violin Bow

One day when Joan was only three years old she accidently tore a pair of Vera's' hose. Little girls always want to be like their moms or their big sisters.

When Vera found out, she whipped Joan severely with the bow to her violin. She kept hitting her and kept hitting her until the violin bow broke. This infuriated Vera so much that she had broken the violin bow. She proceeded to whip Joan even more severely with a hairbrush until the hairbrush broke on Joan's head.

Joan was a tiny little thing. She was small for her age. She had blue eyes. A smile that would light up the room when she smiled and she did a lot of smiling. She was a happy child. She had a twin brother this made her extra special. Joan was also the youngest girl. Every one doted on her. She was tiny and petite for her age. We all carried her around like she was our doll. Vera was a lot bigger.

She towered over all of us. She was the oldest girl.

Now if that was not punishment enough Vera said, "If that does not teach you to leave my things alone I'm going to whip you till you are black and blue all over."

Vera also took Joan's favorite doll and cut the hair off. She ripped the little dolls clothes into shreds. It was a cloth-bodied doll. Vera ripped the cloth body of the doll to shreds also.

Joan cried for her doll for days. This was the last doll our Mother bought Joan. We were all devastated right along with Joan. It was like losing a piece of our Mother all over again. Karen, Debbie, and I cried with Joan.

Joan never did get over the loss of her doll. She kept the doll as a souvenir of sorts, as a reminder of our mother.

Vera's resentment of all her siblings knew no bounds it got wider and scarier with each passing day. We were all terrified of her. It was as if she was obsessed or demon possessed. None of us seemed to matter to her. Nothing seemed to matter to her. She was not interested in others interests, only her own.

She ordered us about as if we were puppets. "Get me this. Go get that. Do this! Do that!" Never once asking or saying please! She never once said thank you! When Vera ordered us to do something, it was just like our dad or grandma ordering us. We did it without ever questioning their motives.

Vera tried to make everyone think she loved the violin. We all thought she did love it. However, when she played, she played as if she was sawing her violin in half. She was demanding it to play music for her. She was very aggressive in her handling of the violin to make it play.

If any of the rest of us wanted to play an instrument, Vera made sure there was only time for her to practice. She made sure we could not take the time to practice.

Karen was the example set for the rest of us. Karen started playing the trumpet. Every time Karen got out her trumpet to practice. Vera would get out her violin. She started playing so loudly you had to cover your ears. She played so violently you would think she was trying to break it. Then she would demand each one of us to watch her play. It was as if we were her private audience. If we did not listen to her playing, we got a beating from her. Vera used terrifying tactics to get us to obey her.

Karen never had time to play or practice her trumpet. According to Vera, two instruments could not play at the same time. Vera also said, "The trumpet was too loud and she was getting a head-ache." It was not fun. If we laughed or snickered when she, Vera made a mis-take, we heard this whack! Vera had hit someone over the head with the violin bow. Oh! How I hated these summer afternoons when nothing else was going on and we had to sit and listen to Vera play the violin.

I dreamed of sneaking away. I never had the guts to just get up and walk away. Occasionally I managed to disappear. Most of the time, I just did not go into the room if Vera was in the room.

Vera resented us all. It seemed that she resented some more than she did others. She wished that we had not been born. She even started telling us her wishes. She would say things like if mom had not had so many children she would still be alive. I could have had a better life if it were not for you. Vera had heard Grandma Lamb say this so often she also started saying it. She really believed this.

This made me very sad. She hated me so much; she wished I had never been born. You see I too wished I had never been born. She thought that if mom and dad had not had so many children there would be better things for her. There would be more money to use for her getting private violin lessons. There would be more money for private swimming lessons. She could have a swimming pool pass.

The one year she did get a swimming pool pass Karen bought one for both of them, by doing odd jobs around the neighborhood. Vera would not dream of working in the neighborhood to earn extra money for herself.

Vera wanted to go to the orchestra and just listen. Instead, she had to go as an usher. There was no extra money for such extravagances. To her this was like working. We thought she was lucky for getting to be an usher. We were never ushers or anything like that. Either way she wanted us all to be as miserable as she was. She felt stuck, helping to watch the children that were not hers.

She was successful too. I avoided her like the plague if she was in the room I was not. If she came into the room, I left. She scared me that much I wanted nothing to do with her.

At every turn, she would slap me on the face. She would punch me on the back. She pinched me as hard as she could without ceasing. I hated it.

This was the toll to pay for her resentment. If you did not do as she wished there was hell to pay.

There were days when there just was no pleasing her. Nothing you did was right. She had nine little brothers and sisters to order about and to abuse. She abused us just as much as our parents did, they taught her to do these things by being abusive themselves.

I did not understand how anyone could hate her own brothers and sisters so much. It just did not make any sense to me.

We were hoping she would change but she never did. She kept us on our toes thinking of ways to avoid her.

The Bean Dinner

We had few activities that were fun. We did not get to go to too many community activities.

There was a community festival that was a lot of fun. The local merchants got together and sponsored it. There were rides. There were prizes for the kids. The kids would get rides for five cents.

The main attraction was the bean soup, thus the name of the community festivities. It was cheap too, only five cents a cup. It was delicious. The women of the neighborhood cooked it. They cooked it all day long. They also made corn bread to go with it. The corn bread was delicious too. In addition, there were hot dogs. What kid does not like hot dogs? My Dad took us to the bean dinner sometimes. Usually grandma took us. We walked down from our house. It was probably about a mile from our house. It was always in the summertime.

They had all kinds of contests for the kids to enter. I had two favorite contests that I liked to enter every year. One was the ponytail contest. The other was the twisting contest. I think I loved the twisting contest best. I was a good twister. My brother John was a good twister too. When you won you usually got five gold dollars. This really made it special. Then we could go on more rides. It was fun! I won just about every year that they had a twisting contest or my brother John won.

The ponytail contest was some-thing else I usually won. I would put my hair into a ponytail. Grandma Lamb taught me how to tie my hair up in rags. First, you would wrap your hair around the rag, and then you would wrap the rest of the rag around your hair. Fixing your hair this way was whole process took a while but the results were great.

The curls looked like long Shirley Temple curls. Grandma Lamb liked teaching this. She thought it showed off her artistic side and it did. I did not win the ponytail contest every time. There was a time or two that Joan won. She was so tiny, petite, and adorable with her ponytail. Everyone thought she was the cutest and she won. Joan would get the five gold dollars. I did not like grandma doing my hair she was too rough and tough.

Another contest they had was a cracker-eating contest. Debbie was best at this. She could eat more crackers than anyone I knew. She did not get a dried out mouth from it either. After eating the crackers, you had to whistle to let the judges know you were finished with your crackers. She always ate the most and was able to whistle first. My mouth was always too dry to whistle. I was not very good at this. She always got five gold dollars too. I tried sometimes but never won at this. It was just so seldom we had money to spend. Debbie did not always win the cracker-eating contest. Sometimes Larry would win. Larry just did not get to go very often, he was always too busy helping dad at the garage.

God made sure each one of us was good at something.

Another two contests they had was the sack races and the wheel barrel contests. These two races were Jimmy's field of expertise. If Jimmy was not winning Larry won. He seemed to be able to run the fastest out of all the kids there. He also seemed to be able to maneuver the wheel barrel between the obstacle course. Between Jimmy and Larry, they seemed to be in competition with each other and either one or the other was always winning. This was another thing I was not very good at. I was not very athletic. It is good to share the wealth.

I do not know how the members of the community felt about our family always winning. We went most years and we won most of the prizes. We just happened to have a large family so it would seem as though we were winning everything.

All these things made it possible for all of us to earn some money and to have a little fun in the process. It was another way for the community to be able to get together, meet, and greet each other.

Nose Dive Stops
and Jack Rabbit Starts

There is a saying 'You must have gotten your driver's license from the Cracker Jack box.' Well for grandma that is almost what happened!

It took her five tries to get her driver's license. The younger people at the licensing bureau did not like the way grandma drove. They always flunked her. Grandma kept going to different licensing bureaus until she found one with an old man who was sweet on her. This man gave her, her driver's license. He was about grandma's age.

Grandma was older when she got her driver's license. She was excited. Now she felt like she could help in the transporting of her daughter's children whenever they needed to go to the doctor's office. When she needed to go to the store grandma could go without asking our dad to take her to the store. She was too proud to ask him for anything. It was a win, win situation for them both. Dad did not have to stop what he was doing to take her to the store.

As soon as grandma got home with her driver's license, she took us all for a ride. It was scary.

Dad always told the story about grandma getting her driver's license. He always said, "Yep it took grandma five tries and five different locations before grandma found a place that had an old man that was sweet on her, for her to get her license." Nevertheless, she found a poor sucker that would give it to her. She scared all the other locations so bad she could not afford to go back to that same place twice. She had to promise to go out and have dinner with the man who finally gave her, her license. Dad would laugh himself silly. He thought it was the funniest thing.

Grandma's driving was scary.

When grandma came up to a traffic light, she would slam on the breaks. This was not a light tap of easing to a stop.

She literally slammed on the breaks. If you were sitting in the front seat, you ended up in the dashboard. If you were in the back seat, your head hit the seat in front of you. It never failed.

When she took off again, her foot slammed into the gas pedal. Then your head hit the back of the seat. If you could have banged your head into the seat, you would have. We did slam our heads into the back of the seat and the seats were not very soft.

No, it was not fun riding with grandma.

Grandma's driving became known as, jackrabbit starts, and nosedive stops. Sometimes the nosedive stops ended up with you having a bloody lip, or bloody nose or forehead with a big knot.

Grandma of course did not think her driving was very bad and was offended. She always defended her driving. She would say things like, "Well I have not hit anyone yet. I did not side swipe any cars."

The side streets that grandma always traveled on were very narrow. She always drove those big Chevys' that were huge. When grandma sat behind the wheel of a car you could barely she her head above the steering wheel and the dashboard because she was so short. Even if grandma put a pillow under her and behind her, which she always did, she could barely see above the steering wheel.

As you went past grandma going, in the opposite direction you had to do a double take to make sure you saw what you saw. Just a little white haired old woman passing you by, in a car too big for her, they did not make little cars back then.

She was an incredible sight! It was hilarious. She was proud of her driver's license though. She drove everywhere whenever possible. Dad never let her drive his car. He felt she was not a safe enough driver to trust her to drive.

Jimmy Gets a Beating

Jimmy was just five years old when he decided to follow his older sibling's example Debbie and Freddie.

Debbie and Freddie looked more like twins than Jimmy and Joan did. Jimmy and Joan were the twins. Debbie and Freddie were inseparable. If you found one you knew the other, one was close by. One day they took their tricycle and rode it down to our dad's garage. We had big tricycles back then in fifty's not the little things fit for preschooler of today. Freddie peddled and Debbie stood on the back end with her arms holding onto Freddie. Anyway, the garage where our dad worked was a good three miles away.

When they got to the garage dad thought it was a great thing. Dad and all his cronies thought it was cute. They raved and raved about it for days and days. Look how cute it was for these two to ride their tricycle down to see their dad at Art's garage. They got candy, pop, and money for their troubles. They were able to earn some money too. All of us were saving pop bottles to earn money.

Heck all Freddie and Debbie had to do to earn some money was ride their tricycle to the garage and they earned extra money. They also had to sweep the garage floor. It was always a greasy mess and they had to pick up some of dad's tools off the floor.

Heck! What kid would not like that idea? We all wanted to earn some extra spending money.

A few days later Jimmy thought, he would do the same thing as his older brother and sister. He wanted to earn money and candy too. Well dad did not think it was funny anymore.

Jimmy got a beating for his trouble. All Jimmy was doing was mimicking what Debbie and Freddie had done and Dad beat him. Dad did not give Jim a light little tap. It was one of those chilly wintry days in the springtime just before summer comes barreling through.

"What the hell are you doing down here," Dad asked Jimmy.

Jimmy said, "I just wanted to come down and earn some money too. I wanted to do what Debbie and Freddie had done a few days ago."

Dad said, "Well you don't come down here, do you hear me." He beat Jimmy with a belt so severely Jimmy peed his pants. Then he got a beating for peeing his pants.

If that was not enough, he pulled Jimmy's pants down to dry them off. Jimmy did not cry though. I do not know how he did not cry but he did not cry. I would have cried. Jimmy was more mad than angry. He could not believe that dad would rave on and on about what Freddie and Debbie had done and then beat him for doing the same thing.

Then dad picked Jimmy up and put him on top of the kerosene heater. He used this to heat the garage, in the winter. Jimmy had burn marks from the heater all over his bottom side. The marks were black that is how bad it burned him. Dad's cronies and his newest light of love was snickering and laughing so hard that this egged Dad on even more.

Dad of course was already drunk.

Dad was trying to get rid of the wet pants, instead he blistered Jimmy's backside.

Jimmy hurt so badly and he was so mad he rode his tricycle back home. Jimmy was the boy who looked like our mother. He had dark hair and brown eyes. He was always looking for a way to earn money. He was sweet natured and protective of his sisters and his younger brother. He had a twin sister. His twin sister had sandy blonde hair and blue eyes. She was a lot tinier than he was too.

Jimmy would do anything to help us when we needed help. If a boy or a girl at school picked on his younger siblings, he was there for the rescue. Sometimes he even helped the older ones when necessary. Jimmy was not very big so he liked to reason with people rather than fight. He liked to talk them out of being mad.

Dad got even madder when he realized Jimmy had ridden his tricycle back home. He drove home taking two older boys (John and Larry) home with him.

Dad left Junior to run the garage business for the rest of the day. Our dad had already been drinking by this time. There was not any reasoning with him. When dad got drunk, he was mean. He did not know what he was doing. He did not seem to care what he was doing. Dad just beat us kids and caroused with the women.

When Jimmy got home he climbed a tree to try to hide from our dad and avoid him. He knew dad could not come out on the tree limb to get him. Dad was too heavy. However, dad did send someone younger and more agile. He sent Larry out to get him. Larry was the only son who did exactly what dad wanted him to, no questions asked. Larry did bring Jimmy down from the tree. Dad beat Jimmy some more. How was Larry to know Dad was going to beat, Jimmy some more. Larry just did not argue.

They never did take Jimmy to the doctors for his blistered bottom. His butt had black marks on it from where dad had put him on the heater. It was red. Blisters were already forming. They had popped open and were bleeding. It was a mass of puss. Dad had taken his belt off. He was beating Jimmy. Dad just kept hitting him and hitting him. Jimmy was only six years old.

When he went back to school, he had trouble sitting down. His nerves from being beaten was shot he started getting the shakes. He became jumpy.

After this Jimmy was black and blue from the tip of his head down to the tip of his toes. He had blisters and welts everywhere you looked. He was bleeding everywhere from where the belt had hit him. As the blood dried his clothes stuck to his body. He was crying now though. Not from the beating so much, as it was from being so mad, that he was too little to stop our dad from being so brutal.

He had two black eyes. No one ever questioned any of this.

He might have been three and a half feet tall weighing in around fifty pounds. Dad was five feet ten and a half inches tall weighing in around two hundred pounds. His hands were hardened and roughened from hard work as a mechanic. He was very strong. Mechanics work makes you this way because of all the heavy lifting you have to do. Therefore, when he got angry his beatings was severe.

When I saw Jimmy, he was not crying anymore. I do not know how Jimmy stood it. He was not crying. I would have been. He was just standing there. Jimmy balled his fist into tight little balls. If you could read his thoughts they were saying, "I will get you back for this old man." No tears, no crying fits no begging for mercy.

I just wanted to go up to him and hide him. Take him somewhere safe. Away from dad, away from the situation but then I would get a beating too. I did nothing but watch and suffer silently. Crying on the inside not showing any emotion. Not letting anyone know I cared. I was afraid to shed real tears. Afraid I too would get a beating if I did.

I sometimes thought my dad was trying to impress his new girlfriend with this display. She was twenty-nine years old. He was forty-seven. She had five kids and he had eleven kids. She was trying to make a good impression. She went around to each one of us kids and asked us what we thought. She said, "Does your dad drink a lot?"

What were we supposed to say? If we said "Yes" than we would have gotten a beating. If we said, "No!" than we were lying and this was confusing to us.

We did not want a beating but that is just the way drunks work. You do not cross drunks and what they want and right now, he wanted this woman. You learn to do as they say or suffer the consequences. The consequences usually involved a beating. It would not have been a light tap either it would have been a full scale all force added beating!

We all took the easy alternative and said, "No, he does not drink." and "Yes! He is a good daddy."

She said, "After we get married I will make sure nothing like this happens again. Nothing like what happened to Jimmy." What kid would not want a stepmother who could make sure you would never got a beating or be hit again.

We were leery. We already had trust issues. We did not even trust our own family members. How were we to trust this stranger?

She said all the right things to make us feel good and important. This woman acted like a kids opinion mattered to her. However, she laughed right along with all Dads cronies, his drunken friends not that the outcome would have been any different. We did not know all of this though. They would have still gotten married. However, we should have been even more leery of this woman.

Then Dad came to each of us separately and asked, "What do you think? Do you like her?" We said, "Yes sir" and "No sir." What do you think we are going to say to a drunk? "Yes we liked her." "Yes she seems nice and likable." "Yes we would like her as a stepmother." The alternative was a beating. You did what he said, when he said it or else. It was scary to me. Dad had never asked my opinion about anything. I was not about to say anything but "Yes" now. I just wanted him to go back to ignoring me. I wanted him to go back to pretending I did not exist. It was easier when dad just existed and was not around.

Karen and I are older now. We are finally able to keep the house clean to Grandma's expectations and specifications. The other kids are older too and are not making as many messes either. They are helping us to keep it clean. This way we can all go outside and play.

Grandma Lamb had gone back to work. She had quit for a little while to help take care of us kids. Grandma realized that in order to put food on the table we needed more money. More than the few coins dad dealt out to her to buy groceries. It took a lot of money to feed this many kids.

Things were finally on an even keel here at the house on Harris Avenue. Grandma is gone a lot because she is working. We stay out of her way when she is home.

Dad is getting married.

Will she be mean?

Will she be nice?

Will things be different?

Epilog

As in my previous book, I hope this book helps those families in need of help.

If you see yourself in any of these situations please seek help. Get family counseling. If you are a parent, please stop the abuse. Your child only wants you to love them.

If you are a child, please seek help from a trusted friend or adviser. Seek help from your teacher. In addition, if you are a child none of this is your fault. Do not take the blame it is not your fault. Do not let your parents blame you.

If you are, a teacher or a person in authority, watch out for these signs of abuse. Help the children who are in your care.

Remember with God, all things are possible. The abuse can stop. One has to actively work at it to stop the abuse. One has to want to raise mentally healthy children.

Do not give up.

Continue to be strong.

God will help you with every step.

You can stop!

Do it before it is too late!

These are some of my childhood memories.

I have attempted to bring them back to life to the best of my abilities. There were many more stories I could have told. These are just a small sampling of our lives with grandma.

Do not forget to watch for the third book in the Tin Train Series.

'514 South Harris Avenue'

I ended this story with a new woman in my dad's life.

Will we get a new stepmother?

Will she be nice?

Will the abuses continue?

Will the abuse stop?

Wait and see!

20104937R00105

Made in the USA
Charleston, SC
27 June 2013